Made in the USA
Middletown, DE
28 March 2020

87423716R00070